HOLLYWOOD

'Welcome to Hollywood, Mr Griffith.' The film director D. W. Griffith liked the California village with its sunny weather, friendly people, and orange trees. 'It's a good place to make a movie,' he thought, and soon the first movie, *In Old California*, was made. It was just seventeen minutes long.

Just over a hundred years later, Hollywood is a very different place, but it's still the home of the movies for millions of people. Hollywood means the stars, from Charlie Chaplin to Brad Pitt, from Vivien Leigh to Penélope Cruz. It means the Oscars, the big film studios, Disney, Hitchcock, and Spielberg. And even today, with films on DVD and on the Internet, Hollywood's exciting story still goes on.

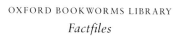

OXFORD BOOKWORMS LIBRARY

Factfiles

Hollywood

Stage 1 (400 headwords)

Factfiles Series Editor: Christine Lindop

JANET HARDY-GOULD

Hollywood

OXFORD UNIVERSITY PRESS

OXFORD
UNIVERSITY PRESS

Great Clarendon Street, Oxford, OX2 6DP, United Kingdom

Oxford University Press is a department of the University of Oxford.
It furthers the University's objective of excellence in research, scholarship,
and education by publishing worldwide. Oxford is a registered trade
mark of Oxford University Press in the UK and in certain other countries

ISBN: 978 0 19 423671 3

A complete recording of *Hollywood* is available on CD. Pack ISBN: 978 0 19 423663 8

Printed in China

Word count (main text): 5,686

For more information on the Oxford Bookworms Library,
visit www.oup.com/elt/gradedreaders

ACKNOWLEDGEMENTS

Cover image: Getty Images (Anne Bancroft and Sidney Poitier at the 1964 Academy Awards/
Julian Wasser/Time Life Pictures)

Maps by: Peter Bull pp.2, 37

The Publishers would like to the thank the following for their permission to reproduce photographs:
Alamy Images pp.8 (kinetoscope/Glasshouse Images), 15 (RKO studios/Pictorial Press Ltd);
Corbis pp.1 (Hollywood sign/Jon Hicks), 11 (Charlie Chaplin/Bettmann Premium), 12 (Rudolph
Valentino/Bettmann), 15 (Bela Lugosi as Dracula/Bettmann), 21 (James Dean/Bettmann),
25 (Star Wars Episode IV/Sunset Boulevard), 32 (2013 Academy Awards/Fairchild Photo
Service/Conde Nast), 33 (Graumann's Chinese Theater/Gavin Hellier/Robert Harding World
Imagery), 38 (Jurassic Park Ride/Louie Psihoyos), 44 (director/Mark Hamilton); Getty Images
pp.7 (Photographer Eadweard Muybridge's study of a horse at full gallop in collotype print/Time
& Life Pictures), 10 (Griffith Directing/Hulton Archive), 31 (Michael Douglas & Catherine Zeta-
Jones/JJeffrey Mayer/WireImage), 39 (man with tablet/Tetra Images), 40 (Robert Pattinson/Jon
Furniss/WireImage), cover (Anne Bancroft and Sidney Poitier at the 1964 Academy Awards/Julian
Wasser/Time Life Pictures); Kobal Collection pp.13 (*The Jazz Singer* 1927/Warner Bros), 17 (*Gone
with the Wind* 1939/Selznick/MGM), 19 (*Casablanca* 1942/Warner Bros), 20 (*The Third Man* 1949/1949
STUDIOCANAL FILMS LTD.), 21 (Marilyn Monroe), 23 (*Jaws* 1975/Universal), 25 (*Independence Day*
1996/20th Century Fox), 26 (*Avatar* 2009/Twentieth Century Fox Film Corporation), 29 (*Sometimes
Happy, Sometimes Sad* 2001/Dharma Productions); Los Angeles Public Library pp.3 (old Hollywood),
5 (old map of Hollywood), 6 (Hollywood Hotel); Oxford University Press pp.44 (employee award/
Corbis), 44 (theatre/Creatas), 44 (actors/Comstock), 44 (costume/Ingram), 44 (audience/Fuse); Rex
Features pp.16 (Ginger Rogers and Fred Astaire, 1936/Courtesy Everett Collection), 28 (Hobbiton
film set/Stephen Barker); Shutterstock pp.34 (Will Smith prints/Ritu Manoj Jethani/Shutterstock.
com), 35 (Hollywood walk/Andrew Zarivny/Shutterstock.com); The Bruce Torrence Hollywood
Photograph Collection p.4 (Daeida Wilcox).

CONTENTS

INTRODUCTION   i

1   The place and the movies   1
2   The village   3
3   The early days   7
4   The big studios   13
5   Changes at the studios   18
6   New Hollywood   23
7   Outside Hollywood   27
8   The Oscars   30
9   Grauman's Chinese Theatre   33
10 A visit to Hollywood   36
11 Changing Hollywood   39

GLOSSARY   41
ACTIVITIES: Before Reading   44
ACTIVITIES: While Reading   45
ACTIVITIES: After Reading   49
ABOUT THE AUTHOR   52
ABOUT THE BOOKWORMS LIBRARY   53

1　The place and the movies

What do you think of when you hear the word 'Hollywood'? Do you think of wonderful films like *Lord of the Rings, Star Wars, Titanic,* or *Gone with the Wind?* Or exciting film stars like Johnny Depp, Will Smith, and Marilyn Monroe? Perhaps you remember the Hollywood sign in big letters in the hills or you think of famous roads like Sunset Boulevard or Hollywood Boulevard.

Hollywood is different things to different people. Firstly, it is a place in California in the west of the United States. But it is not a town, it is part of the big city of Los Angeles.

Los Angeles is the second biggest city in the United States and it has nearly four million people. About 200,000 of them live in Hollywood in the northwest of the city.

Of course, Hollywood is not only a place. When we talk about a new Hollywood movie or the latest Hollywood star, we are talking about the American film industry. It is the most famous film industry in the world with a long and interesting story. Today, most movies are made near Hollywood, not in it. But everybody calls them Hollywood films (and 'films' and 'movies' are the same thing).

Hollywood is not only famous for films. It is an important place for the music, television, and radio industry. The television show *Hannah Montana* with the singer Miley Cyrus was made at a TV studio in Hollywood.

The movie industry began in Hollywood in the early twentieth century. Film makers came from across the United States and made films here. But why did people first move to Hollywood? What was different about this small place in California?

2   The village

Today, Hollywood is a part of Los Angeles with many cars, shops, and hotels. But in 1853, there was nothing here, only one small house and lots of tall cactuses. At first, this place had the name Nopalera, after the many Nopal cactus plants here.

By 1870, farmers began to move to the area and they called it the Cahuenga Valley. This part of California is famous for its nice weather. The Santa Monica mountains to the north stop the wind. There are more than 260 days of sun every year but only thirty-seven days of rain. It is not cold in winter and it does not usually go under 7 °C here.

Early days in Hollywood

These early farmers brought orange and other trees with them and the trees did well in the warm sun here. Soon, more people heard about the beautiful Cahuenga Valley and its wonderful weather.

One man, Harvey Wilcox, and his wife Daeida, often visited the area on a Sunday. They loved the quiet roads with their green trees. Harvey bought land in the valley and he made it into smaller parts. He wanted to sell the land to people for houses.

In early 1887, Daeida went to see her family in a different part of the United States. On her visit, she met a woman. This woman talked happily about her home and her land near Chicago – it was called Hollywood. Daeida loved this name and she could not forget it.

Daeida Wilcox

When Daeida arrived home, she told Harvey about it at once. Harvey liked the name too so he gave the name Hollywood to their land in the Cahuenga Valley. And so Hollywood got its name, people think.

By 1900, 500 people lived in the area and there was a small hotel, some shops, and a newspaper, *The Cahuenga Suburban*. The most important street was called Prospect Avenue. It was a quiet street with trees and gardens along it.

In 1903, a bigger and more beautiful hotel was built. This was the famous Hollywood Hotel, and it had thirty-three rooms for visitors. Soon, rich people came to the area. They bought land and built nice houses with wonderful gardens.

Of course, all these gardens and trees needed water and Hollywood did not have much at this time. So in 1910, the area became a part of Los Angeles and it began to take some of its water from the city. At this time, Prospect Avenue changed its name to Hollywood Boulevard.

By 1910, 5,000 people lived in the village of Hollywood. But soon new people arrived from all over the United States and other parts of the world. What did they want and why did they come here?

3 The early days

The story of the moving picture began in the late nineteenth century with a number of different inventions. In June 1878, a British man called Eadweard Muybridge made a moving picture of a horse in Palo Alto, California. In the early 1890s, W. K. L. Dickson and Thomas Edison of the New York Edison Company made two inventions, the Kinetograph and the Kinetoscope. The Kinetograph was a big moving picture camera and the Kinetoscope projected the moving pictures in a box. But only one person at a time could watch these pictures.

Muybridge's photos

Soon after, in March 1895, the Lumière brothers showed people in France a new invention, the Cinématographe. This was a moving picture camera, but it recorded and projected the moving pictures too. It was better than the Kinetograph because it was smaller and a lot of people could watch the pictures at once.

The new moving pictures or 'movies' were very popular. At first, people watched them in places like hotels or shops. The movies were not very long, they were often under a minute! In the 1895 film *The Sea* by the Lumière brothers, there were moving pictures of people in the sea. The movie was only 38 seconds long!

Looking into a Kinetoscope

By the early 1900s, there were better moving picture inventions and a number of these were under the name of the New York Edison Company. But people needed to give money to Edison when they used their new cameras or projectors. When film makers worked in the New York area, men from the Edison Company sometimes arrived and took away their cameras! So people in the early film industry moved far from New York to places like California.

In 1910, the director D. W. Griffith from the Biograph film company of New York came to California with some famous actors – Lionel Barrymore, Mary Pickford, and Lillian Gish. He made a film in Los Angeles but he looked for other interesting places too.

One day, Griffith visited the village of Hollywood. It was a truly wonderful place for a film, he thought. The people were friendly to film makers, the weather was good, and there were interesting things near here too like hills and mountains.

Griffith made the first movie in Hollywood in February 1910. It was about California in the nineteenth century and it was called *In Old California*. Like all films at this time, it was a silent movie – actors did not speak in films for another twenty years. At seventeen minutes, it was not very long but it had a story!

Other film makers learned about Hollywood and the first film studio was built on Sunset Boulevard in 1911 by the Nestor Motion Picture Company. The director Cecil B. DeMille opened a studio in Hollywood in 1913.

In 1914 DeMille made the first Hollywood feature film – a long film with a story. It was called *The Squaw Man* and it was seventy-four minutes long. The movie was made for 15,000 dollars but it made nearly 250,000 dollars in the new movie theaters across the country. There was money in these moving pictures! People quickly understood this.

Everybody loved the silent movies; the stories were easy and there was exciting music too. People could not hear the actors speak but they could often read their words under the pictures.

Director D. W. Griffith (in white hat) making a film

Soon, actors and directors from across the world came to Hollywood. One young British actor, Charlie Chaplin, arrived here in the spring of 1913 and his first film *Making a Living* came out in 1914. In his next film, people met Chaplin's famous character 'the Tramp' with his big trousers, small coat, and black hat. Everybody laughed at his sorry face.

The Tramp was a very popular silent movie character and Chaplin became famous all over the world. But he was not only an actor – he wrote stories and music for films, and he was a director too. Chaplin opened a studio in Hollywood in 1917 and many of his movies like *The Gold Rush* of 1925 were filmed here.

In 1917, a 22-year-old Italian man came to Hollywood. Directors liked his wonderful dark hair and his beautiful

Chaplin as the Tramp

brown eyes, and he soon had small parts in silent movies. In the 1920s, he was the star of popular films like *Blood and Sand*. Women all over the world loved him and they cried at his films. What was his name? Rudolph Valentino!

Valentino was one of the first movie stars. Photographers ran after him in the street and his picture was always in the newspapers. He lived like a true Hollywood star and often stayed in the Hollywood Hotel, always in room number 264!

In 1918, a company built expensive houses on the hills near Hollywood Boulevard. This was Whitley Heights, the world's first village for the stars. Valentino moved here in 1922 and it was later home to many famous people.

But in August 1926, Valentino suddenly became ill and died. He was only thirty-one years old. When his body went through the streets of New York, 100,000 people came and said goodbye. Friends later brought his body home to the cemetery in Hollywood.

By 1925, 130,000 people lived in Hollywood and over 800 movies were made here every year. Nearly all films

were black and white in the 1920s, but the first color Hollywood feature film *The Toll of the Sea* came out in 1922. People could see the actors in color but they still could not hear their voices. But in 1927, things changed and many actors were not happy!

Rudolph Valentino

4   The big studios

In 1927, the big Hollywood movie was *The Jazz Singer* with actor Al Jolson. Across the United States, film directors talked about it, newspapers wrote about it, and everybody wanted to see it. But what was important about this new film?

When people went to see *The Jazz Singer*, they could hear the actors' voices. It was one of the first 'talkies' and it changed the movie world. Directors did not suddenly stop making silent films, but by 1929, most Hollywood studios made talkies.

For silent movie actors the change was not easy. Some had bad voices and others could not remember their words. A number of silent stars lost all their work and never made a film again. Later, the wonderful 2011 French film *The Artist* looked back at this time in Hollywood.

The RKO Studio

By the late 1920s, there were twenty film studios in Hollywood. The most important were called 'the Big Five'. They were Twentieth Century Fox, MGM, RKO, Warner Bros., and Paramount Pictures. They owned buildings in Hollywood but they began to build studios in the valleys near here too.

These studios were very important at this time. They made about 90 per cent of the feature films in the United States and they owned nearly all the movie theaters too. When Paramount opened a new movie theater, for example, that theater could only show Paramount films.

The studios often showed films for the first time at Hollywood movie theaters. These first nights or 'premieres' were sometimes at the famous Grauman's Chinese Theatre on Hollywood Boulevard. Like many movie theaters, it was beautiful and *very* big; 2,258 people could watch movies there.

The studios had long contracts with their stars, and actors often stayed with their studio for years. MGM had the actors Clark Gable, Jean Harlow, and Greta Garbo. When people saw them in a film, they understood at once – it was an MGM movie.

Thousands of people worked for the studios – writers, directors, drivers, builders, and of course actors. There were famous stars, and also extras – actors with very small parts. The director Cecil B. DeMille was famous for his epics – long, expensive films with lots of music and hundreds of extras, like his film *Cleopatra* in 1934.

People from across the world came to Hollywood. They all wanted one thing – to become a film star! They worked in old hotels or cheap shops and then looked for work in the movies. Many went to a company called Central Casting on Hollywood Boulevard. Central Casting found extras for all the big films. In the late 1920s, the names of 17,000 people were on its books.

The world of Hollywood was not easy. Only a small number of directors and stars made a lot of money. In the early 1930s, there was the Great Depression in the United States. Companies closed and people were without work. At first, things were not bad in Hollywood but by 1933, shops and hotels closed here too.

But movie theaters were popular in the Great Depression. When audiences watched a movie they could forget everything for an hour or two. There were different types of films. Every type had its usual story and audiences understood these. One type of movie was the horror film. People loved to feel afraid when they saw these!

Bela Lugosi

In 1931, the first big talkie horror film came out. It was *Dracula* with the Hungarian actor Bela Lugosi. His dark eyes, white face, and slow, cold voice became famous and soon he was the star of many Hollywood horror films like *Son of Frankenstein.*

In the 1930s, Hollywood made musicals – films with music and singing too. Two famous actors in musicals were Fred Astaire and Ginger Rogers. But they did not only sing, they danced beautifully too. Their 1935 film *Top Hat* has one of the most famous dances in the story of Hollywood.

Fred and Ginger

Not all Hollywood films had actors in them. A young man called Walt Disney moved to Hollywood in 1923 and opened a cartoon studio. He made small black and white cartoons here with his brother.

In 1934, they began a new type of cartoon, a color feature film called *Snow White and the Seven Dwarfs.* They finished the film three years later, in 1937. When it came out, the audiences loved everything about it – the music, the story, and the beautiful colors.

Two big color movies opened in 1939. One was the MGM film *The Wizard of Oz.* The story came from a popular book by L. Frank Baum and it was made into a musical with actress Judy Garland. Her character, Dorothy, wore famous red shoes in the film.

The actors in this movie all had exciting costumes and make-up. Many of them needed to arrive at the MGM studios at five o'clock every morning and stay for hours in the costume and make-up area!

The second film came from a book too – *Gone with the Wind* by Margaret Mitchell. The movie was about the war in the United States in the nineteenth century (1861–65) and it was a true epic. It had fifty actors with speaking parts, 2,400 extras, 1,100 horses, *and* it was three hours and fifty-eight minutes long!

Millions of people saw Vivien Leigh and Clark Gable in this exciting love story. At the time, *Gone with the Wind* was the longest feature film and it made more money than any other film too.

1939 was the best year for films from Hollywood studios, people say. But in the 1940s the part played by the studios changed.

Gone with the Wind

5 Changes at the studios

The Second World War from 1939 to 1945 was important in the story of Hollywood. In the years before the war many European people from Jewish families arrived here because of problems in their countries. Two of these were the directors Fritz Lang and Billy Wilder.

Between 1939 and 1945 Hollywood made lots of war movies. People can easily forget most of these but everybody remembers one black and white film. This is *Casablanca* from 1942 with Humphrey Bogart and the Swedish actress Ingrid Bergman. It is a love story in the dark world of war.

Not all movies were about war. One 1941 film, *Citizen Kane*, was about Charles Foster Kane, a rich newspaper owner. Many people call it the best Hollywood film of all time. The writer, director, and most important actor was Orson Welles. He was only twenty-five years old!

Hollywood moved away from the happy films of the 1930s. The new movies were often detective stories with bad, cold characters. They were made in black and white with the actors' faces sometimes half in the dark. People later called this type of movie 'film noir'.

One film noir was the 1946 movie *Notorious* with Ingrid Bergman and Cary Grant. This exciting film or

'thriller' had a British director, Alfred Hitchcock. He made many Hollywood thrillers and he was famous for his very small part in every film.

In 1948, the US government made a big change in the film industry. Studios could not own movie theaters

Film noir

and show only their films in them. From this time, the studios stopped making lots of films every year and they stopped their long contracts with the big stars too. This was the end of the wonderful days for the Hollywood studios.

The studios had a different problem too. This time it was not the government. It was a new thing in people's houses – the television. In 1950, about six million US homes had a TV and by 1960 60 million homes had one. Now, some people stopped going to the movies every week.

Many old Hollywood film studios began to make TV shows. Some studios made bigger, more exciting films too, all in wonderful color. And epics were popular again. In 1959, there was the 15 million dollar movie *Ben-Hur* about Rome long ago. It was by the director William Wyler. This movie with actor Charlton

Marilyn Monroe

Heston was made over seven years with 8,000 extras and 100,000 costumes!

In the 1950s, people wanted to forget the dark war years. They were interested in happy films again like Disney's 1950 cartoon *Cinderella* or the 1952 musical *Singin' in the Rain* with actor Gene Kelly.

In 1959, audiences laughed for hours at *Some Like it Hot* by director Billy Wilder. The film had the actors Tony Curtis and Jack Lemmon and a beautiful 32-year-old actress, Marilyn Monroe. She became one of the most famous faces of Hollywood, but died in 1962 when she was only thirty-six.

Other Hollywood stars died young too. One actor, James Dean, was called 'the first American teenager'. He was in only three films, most importantly the 1955 movie *Rebel Without a Cause*. But he died suddenly in a car accident before the film came out. He was twenty-four years old.

James Dean

Music for teenagers became a new industry. Music companies opened in Hollywood and studios soon made movies with singers like Elvis Presley. Excited teenagers stood and danced in movie theaters when they saw his films like *Jailhouse Rock* in 1957.

But the 1960s was a bad time for the Hollywood film industry. The expensive 1963 epic *Cleopatra* with Richard Burton and Elizabeth Taylor lost a lot of money and that year was the worst for the US film industry. Only 121 films were made.

Many old Hollywood studios had money problems and they sold their buildings, land, and wonderful costumes too. In 1970, MGM sold two of Dorothy's beautiful red shoes from *The Wizard of Oz* for 15,000 dollars.

By the 1970s Hollywood was a different place from the 1940s. A big road now went through the area and the Whitley Heights village was in two halves. Many old buildings were no longer there. In 1956, builders took down the Hollywood Hotel, once home to Rudolph Valentino.

When visitors came to Hollywood in the 1970s, many did not like the area. They found dirty streets, bad hotels, and cheap shops. Most film stars now lived in other parts of Los Angeles like Beverly Hills. The old world of Hollywood was dead.

6   New Hollywood

By 1970, there was only one big film studio in Hollywood. That was Paramount Pictures. All the others were in places in the Los Angeles area like Burbank.

In the 1970s, new directors came to Hollywood like Francis Ford Coppola, Martin Scorsese, and George Lucas. They went to film school and they were interested in Italian and French movies from the 1960s.

One young director, Steven Spielberg, made a thriller called *Jaws* about a shark in the sea near a small American town. This 1975 film was very expensive at 9 million dollars. It came out at a popular time of year – the summer – and it opened in about 450 movie theaters at once. *Jaws* was a new type of film – a 'blockbuster'. These films need a lot of money – but they make a lot of money too, and are very popular.

One 1977 blockbuster changed the film world. This was the science fiction movie *Star Wars* by George Lucas.

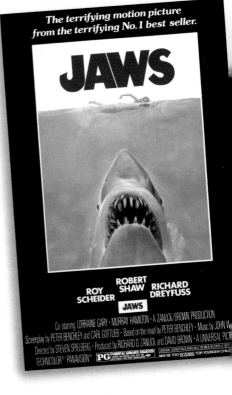

Star Wars

It became famous for its characters and special effects. Many of these special effects were made with computers and people called these moving pictures 'computer-generated imagery' or CGI.

After audiences saw *Star Wars* they could go to the shops and buy *Star Wars* things too. It was one of the first films with merchandizing. There were *Star Wars* pens, watches, clocks, bags, and many other things!

In 1972 the Philips company began to sell home video recorders for about 2,000 dollars and families could watch Hollywood movies at home. Home videos made lots of money for the movie industry. When Steven Spielberg's 1982 blockbuster *E.T. the Extra-Terrestrial* went to video, it made more than 75 million dollars in the United States.

One type of movie had merchandizing and was very popular on video. This was the superhero film, like the blockbusters *Superman* in 1978 and *Superman II* in 1980. Later, in 1989, there was the first of a number of big *Batman* films, and in the 2000s the *X-Men* movies.

In the 1990s, there were big changes in the movie world. Firstly, many movie theaters had a number of rooms now and they could show more than one film at once. This was called a 'multiplex'. The world's biggest multiplex opened in Madrid, Spain in 1998. It could show twenty-five different films at once, to 9,200 people!

New digital technology was important for film makers. Directors could now put Hollywood actors into old films. The 1994 film *Forrest Gump* showed Tom Hanks with famous people from earlier times like John F. Kennedy. Other movies like the 1996 science fiction film *Independence Day* were made truly exciting with CGI pictures too.

The biggest 1990s movie was *Titanic*. This 1997 blockbuster by director James Cameron with Leonardo DiCaprio and Kate Winslet told the story of the last days of the ship the *Titanic*. It was then Hollywood's most expensive film of all time at about 200 million dollars, and it made the most money too, 1.8 billion dollars across the world.

Digital technology came into the home too in the late 1990s. People stopped using videos and they bought DVD players. DVDs had a better picture and often showed more things from the film.

Independence Day

Cartoons changed with the new technology and studios began to make cartoons with computers in the late 1990s and 2000s. There were the four *Shrek* films all with the exciting *Shrek* characters, the *Toy Story* films, and *Finding Nemo*.

When a movie was popular like *Shrek*, the studios often made a film series – a number of different films about the characters. Other film series at this time were *Pirates of the Caribbean*, *Harry Potter,* and *The Twilight Saga*.

In the early years of the twenty-first century film companies made more movies in 3D. Of course, 3D technology was not new. Audiences watched 3D films in the 1950s but the 3D glasses were not very good and people could not see the 3D pictures well.

In 2009, everybody wanted to see one film in 3D, James Cameron's science fiction movie *Avatar*. After only three weeks, it made more money than his earlier blockbuster *Titanic*. 3D films are not always popular with audiences, but some movie companies like them very much. Are there going to be a lot of 3D films in the future? We can only wait and see.

Avatar

7 Outside Hollywood

Not all Hollywood films are made in the United States. Directors sometimes take their actors to a different country because it is important for the story. In the 1950s, there were Hollywood films in cities like Paris or Rome, for example, the 1953 love story *Roman Holiday* with Gregory Peck and Audrey Hepburn.

Other directors are looking for a good place for their science fiction film or horror movie and they find this place in a different country. Parts of four *Star Wars* films were filmed in Tunisia, the three *Lord of the Rings* movies were made in New Zealand, some of *The Bourne Legacy* was filmed in South Korea, and parts of *The Twilight Saga: Breaking Dawn* were made in Brazil.

Sometimes Hollywood movie companies go to other countries because it is cheaper. Some governments want to bring film makers to their country because it gives work to their film industry. These governments often give money to the movie companies when they make films in their countries. Some Hollywood films are now filmed in Canada or perhaps Australia, Hungary, Germany, or the UK.

The US film industry makes about five hundred films every year, but it is not the world's biggest film maker. India makes more than a thousand feature films every year and many of these are made in 'Bollywood'.

The village of Hobbiton, in *Lord of the Rings*

Bollywood is not a place, it is the name for the film industry in Mumbai, the biggest city in India. In Bollywood films people speak in Hindi. People began to use the name Bollywood in the 1970s and it comes from two different words. These are Bombay, the old name for Mumbai, and Hollywood.

Bollywood films are very popular in India and other countries. In 2009 people across the world bought 3.6 million tickets for Bollywood films. In that year, people bought 2.6 million tickets for Hollywood films.

Bollywood films are different from Hollywood films because there is always music and singing in them. When a new Bollywood movie comes out, people often buy the music and listen to it at home.

In India and other countries, Bollywood film stars are more important than any Hollywood stars. For example, the actor Shah Rukh Khan is in more than seventy Bollywood films and he is one of the biggest stars in India.

Shah Rukh Khan with the actress Kajol

8 The Oscars

Every year in late February or early March, movie stars come to the Dolby Theatre on Hollywood Boulevard. The women wear beautiful dresses and the men put on expensive suits. Hundreds of photographers take pictures of them when they walk slowly into the theater. Why are they here? It is time for the Oscar award ceremony!

The true name of the Oscar ceremony is the Academy Awards Ceremony. In the 1920s, a number of important Hollywood people wanted to give awards in the new world of film and they had their first ceremony in 1929. They gave out fifteen statuettes. These were later called Oscars.

Now, there are more than twenty Oscars. The most famous Oscars are for the best actor and best actress, and the best picture. But there are other Oscars, for example, for the best costumes, and best hair and make-up too.

Katharine Hepburn has the most Best Actress Oscars with four, and Daniel Day-Lewis has the most Best Actor Oscars with three. The films with the most Oscars are *Ben-Hur*, *Titanic*, and *The Lord of the Rings*, all with eleven Oscars. The oldest and youngest winners of an Oscar for acting are Christopher Plummer, at eighty-two, and Tatum O'Neal, at ten.

One Oscar is for the Best Foreign Language Film – for films not in English. Italy is the country with the most movies with this Oscar. For example, the film *Life Is Beautiful* won the 1998 Oscar. Other movies with this Oscar are *All About My Mother* by Spanish director Pedro Almodóvar, *Kolya* by Czech director Jan Svěrák, and *Okuribito* by Japanese director Takita Yōjirō.

When a person wins an Oscar, they come to the front of the theater and take the Oscar statuette. Of course, the winners then need to say something – make a speech! Actress Greer Garson gave the longest speech in 1943 at

Michael Douglas and Catherine Zeta Jones at the Oscars, 2013

five and a half minutes. Now the winners cannot speak for longer than forty-five seconds. The quickest speeches were from actor William Holden in 1954 and director Alfred Hitchcock in 1968. They said two words: 'Thank you'!

Ben Affleck and George Clooney with their Oscars, 2013

9   Grauman's Chinese Theatre

Grauman's Chinese Theatre at 6925 Hollywood Boulevard is perhaps the most famous of the 'old Hollywood' places. Its name comes from Sid Grauman, one of its first owners. Grauman opened it in 1927 with the film stars Douglas Fairbanks and Mary Pickford. In 2013 it changed its name to TCL Chinese Theatre, but many people use the old name.

Visitors to Grauman's always go to the front of the movie theater. There outside the building they can see the names and prints of nearly 200 famous people in concrete. They are mostly prints of hands and feet.

There are different stories about the first footprint. One is about a star of silent films called Norma Talmadge, a friend of Sid Grauman's. One day in 1927, she stopped her car in front of the theater and she put her foot into some new concrete by accident. This made a footprint. Soon after, Sid Grauman began to ask other stars for their footprints in ceremonies at the theater.

Later, there were the prints of stars and directors like Cecil B. DeMille 1941, John Wayne 1950, Marilyn Monroe 1953, Tom Cruise 1992, Samuel L. Jackson 2006, and Robert Pattinson and other *Twilight* actors in 2011.

Some prints are a little different. Betty Grable left the print of her famously beautiful legs in 1943, and Whoopi Goldberg did a print of her hair in 1995. There are the 1984 prints of the Disney character Donald Duck and his 'voice' Clarence Nash too!

Many visitors to Grauman's take photos of the famous sidewalk along Hollywood Boulevard and Vine Street too. This is called the Hollywood Walk of Fame. There are more than 2,400 stars with people's names along 2.1 kilometres of sidewalk.

The stars are for singers, actors, directors, and people from the early days of moving pictures, like Thomas Edison and the Lumière brothers. And there are stars for animal actors, like Lassie the dog!

When a famous person dies, people come to their star on the Hollywood Walk of Fame. When Elizabeth Taylor died on 23 March 2011 people put flowers and photographs on her star.

10 A visit to Hollywood

Hollywood is now a nicer place than in the 1970s and millions of people come here every year. In some streets, visitors can look up and see the famous Hollywood sign, 14 metres tall. This was built in 1923 on Mount Lee, part of the Hollywood Hills.

It was a sign for an area of new houses and at first it said 'Hollywoodland'. But in 1949, it lost 'land' and became 'Hollywood'. Over the years the sign became very old, so in 1978 a number of film stars gave a lot of money for it. Now it looks better again.

Visitors interested in Hollywood stars go to the Hollywood Forever Cemetery. Many actors and directors are here like Douglas Fairbanks, Cecil B. DeMille, Norma Talmadge, and Rudolph Valentino.

There are famous stories about Valentino. After he died on 23 August 1926, a woman in a black dress visited the cemetery every year on 23 August. She put red flowers on Valentino's name.

You can find wonderful photos of old Hollywood at the Lasky-DeMille Barn. This studio is important because DeMille made the first Hollywood feature film here in 1914. It is across the street from the Hollywood Bowl. There you can sit and listen to music under the night sky.

A visit to Universal Studios

For families, there is Universal Studios near Hollywood. It has over four million visitors every year. Universal is a working film studio, but there are many other things to do and see. When visitors arrive they sit on a little train and then go through different places from famous films, like Hitchcock's *Psycho* and Spielberg's *War of the Worlds*.

Often visitors want to see movie stars but this is not always easy. Many do not live in Hollywood. When they go out, they often arrive in a car with black windows. Perhaps the best times to see them are premieres or the ceremonies for a new star on the Hollywood Walk of Fame.

11   Changing Hollywood

In the early 1900s, nobody knew about the quiet village of Hollywood. But in 1910 the first film makers arrived and then the studios opened. By the 1920s, it was more famous for movies than any other place. Soon, when people talked about the American film industry, they said one word – Hollywood.

Over a hundred years after Hollywood began, its films never stop being popular. In 2011, Hollywood films sold 32.6 billion dollars in movie theater tickets across the world. Hollywood movies are becoming more popular in countries like China with 2 billion dollars in tickets sold there in that year.

But of course, Hollywood has problems too. People do not always watch films at the movie theater, on TV, or on DVD now. Some watch the latest Hollywood films on the internet, and sometimes this is free. This loses Hollywood billions of dollars, some people say, and it is very bad for the movie industry in the years to come.

But Hollywood is built on a long and truly wonderful story of famous actors, directors, and film studios and it is not going to stop any time soon!

GLOSSARY

actor (for a woman sometimes **actress**) a person whose job is acting in films or plays

area a part of a town or country

audience the people who are watching a film, play, concert, etc.

award a prize that you give to somebody who has done something very well

become to grow or change and begin to be something

build to make something by putting parts together

buy to give money for something

cactus a plant with a lot of sharp points that grows in hot dry places

cemetery an area of ground where dead people are put under the earth

century a time of 100 years

ceremony an important time when people come to a special place or building to do traditional things

CGI (computer-generated imagery) the use in films of pictures made on a computer

character a person in a film or story

come out to be in cinemas or movie theaters for the first time

company a group of people who work together to make or sell things

contract an official piece of paper that says that somebody agrees to do something

costume the special clothes that an actor wears in a film

digital technology machines that allow you to record, change, and add to films

director the person who tells the actors in a film what to do

extra (*n*) a person who has a very small part in a film

farmer a person who keeps animals and grows food

glasses something you wear on your face to help you to see better

government a group of people who control a country

Great Depression a time in the 1930s when many people had
  no jobs

horse a big animal that can carry people and pull heavy things

industry all the companies that make the same thing

invention a thing that somebody has made for the first time

land a piece of ground

make-up colors and powders that actors put on their faces to
  change the way they look

merchandizing things you can buy that are connected with a
  popular film

mountain a very high hill

movie theater a building where you go to see movies

music when you sing or play an instrument, you make music

newspaper people read about things that happen every day in this

other different

own (*v*) to have something that is yours

part one of the pieces of something; the job of being a character
  in a film

place where something or somebody is

popular liked by a lot of people

premiere the first time that a film is shown to people

problem something that is difficult

project to show a film onto a screen; (*n*) **projector**

record to make a copy of a film so that you can watch it again;
  (*n*) **recorder**

science fiction a kind of film about life in the future or on other
  planets

sell to give something to someone and get money for it

show (*n & v*) to put something where people can see it; a
  program on TV

special effects exciting things in films that are made by computers
  or by special photography

star a famous and popular actor; the most important actor in a
  film; a sign like this ★

story words that tell you about what happened in a certain place or time

studio a place where films are made

teenager a person between thirteen and nineteen years old

type a group of things that are the same in some way

use to do a job with something

valley a low piece of land between hills or mountains

voice the sounds you make with your mouth when you speak

war fighting between countries or groups of people

win to be the best at something

world the earth with all its countries and people

ACTIVITIES

Before Reading

1 **Match the words to the pictures. You can use a dictionary.**

1 ☐ actors   2 ☐ audience   3 ☐ award
4 ☐ costume   5 ☐ director   6 ☐ movie theater

2 **What do you know about Hollywood? Circle the correct words.**

Hollywood is on the *west / east* coast of the United States and it is part of the city of *Miami / Los Angeles*. About *20,000 / 200,000* people live there now.

In the early *19th / 20th* century a lot of film makers arrived in Hollywood. They liked the nice *weather / houses* there and they soon began to make films. By the year 1925, *80 / 800* movies were made every year in Hollywood.

ACTIVITIES

While Reading

Read Chapter 1. Then rewrite these untrue sentences with the correct information.

1 Sunset Boulevard is the name of a hill in Hollywood.
2 Hollywood is part of a small town in California.
3 Los Angeles is the third biggest city in the US.
4 Hollywood is in the southwest of Los Angeles.
5 'Hollywood' is the name of the American car industry.
6 Today, most new movies are made in Hollywood.
7 The movie industry began in the late twentieth century.

Read Chapter 2. Then circle *a*, *b*, or *c*.

1 In 1853, there was one _____ in this part of California.
   a) farm   b) hotel   c) house
2 This area is famous for its ____.
   a) cold wind   b) warm days with sun   c) small cactuses
3 Harvey Wilcox wanted to sell land for _____.
   a) houses   b) farms   c) shops
4 Daeida first heard about the name 'Hollywood' in _____.
   a) 1870   b) 1887   c) 1900
5 In 1903, a _____ was built for visitors to Hollywood.
   a) beautiful shop   b) water garden   c) nice hotel
6 At this time, Hollywood did not have a lot of ____.
   a) water   b) orange trees   c) gardens
7 _____ people had their home in Hollywood by 1910.
   a) 50   b) 500   c) 5,000

Read Chapter 3. Then match these halves of sentences.

1 In Muybridge's early moving picture, you could see . . .
2 Dickson and Edison made a moving picture camera called . . .
3 The smaller Cinématographe camera was made . . .
4 People in the early film industry moved away from . . .
5 The first movie in Hollywood was made . . .
6 The first Hollywood film studio was built . . .
7 Charlie Chaplin came to Hollywood . . .
8 The first feature film in color came out . . .

a New York.
b by the Lumière brothers.
c a horse.
d in 1922.
e in 1911.
f by D. W. Griffith.
g the Kinetograph.
h in early 1913.

Read Chapter 4. Choose the best question-word for these questions, and then answer them.

How many / When / Where / Who / Why

1 . . . did everybody want to see *The Jazz Singer*?
2 . . . big Hollywood film studios were there in the late 1920s?
3 . . . could people see many of the important film premieres?
4 . . . was famous for his epics with lots of extras?
5 . . . did the first important 'talkie' horror movie come out?
6 . . . came to Hollywood and made cartoons?
7 . . . extras were in the epic film *Gone with the Wind*?

Read Chapter 5. Then fill in the gaps with these numbers.

24, 25, 32, 1942, 1948, the 1970s, 60 million

1 The movie *Casablanca* came out in _____.
2 Orson Welles made *Citizen Kane* when he was _____.
3 There were big changes in the movie industry in _____.
4 _____ American homes had a TV in 1960.
5 Marilyn Monroe was _____ years old in *Some Like it Hot*.
6 The actor James Dean died when he was _____.
7 Many visitors did not like Hollywood in _____.

Read Chapter 6. Then answer these questions.

1 Why was *Jaws* an important film?
2 How did *Star Wars* change the film world?
3 How much were the early home video recorders?
4 What were early examples of superhero blockbusters?
5 How much money did *Titanic* make across the world?
6 When did people first begin watching 3D movies?

Read Chapter 7. Are these sentences true (T) or false (F)? Rewrite the false ones with the correct information.

1 Parts of the *Star Wars* movies were filmed in New Zealand.
2 Some Hollywood movies are filmed in Canada.
3 The US film industry is the world's biggest film maker.
4 People first talked about 'Bollywood' in the 1970s.
5 Bollywood films are only popular in India.
6 Shah Rukh Khan is in over seventy Bollywood films.

Read Chapter 8. Then circle the correct words.

1 The first Academy Award Ceremony was in *1920 / 1929*.
2 At first, there were *fifteen / twenty* statuettes.
3 Tatum O'Neal was *ten / eleven* when she won an Oscar.
4 Greer Garson made the *quickest / longest* Oscar speech.

Read Chapter 9. Then fill in the gaps with these names.

Whoopi Goldberg / Sid Grauman / Lassie / John Wayne

1 The famous movie theater's name comes from _____.
2 In 1950, _____ left his prints at the theater.
3 _____ made prints of her hair in 1995.
4 Many people have sidewalk stars, and ____ has one too!

Read Chapter 10. Write the places next to the sentences.

Hollywood Bowl, Lasky-DeMille Barn, Mount Lee,
The Walk of Fame, Universal Studios

1 You can see the Hollywood sign here. _____
2 You can look at old pictures of Hollywood here. _____
3 You can hear wonderful music here. _____
4 You can see things from movies like *Psycho* here. _____
5 Perhaps you can see a film star here. _____

Read Chapter 11. Answer the questions.

1 Where are Hollywood movies becoming more popular?
2 What problems does Hollywood have now?

ACTIVITIES

After Reading

1 **Complete the crossword.**

Across

2 Hollywood's first name 'Nopalera' came from this plant.

6 One of the earliest moving pictures in 1878 showed a _____.

8 *Titanic* was an important film in the late 20th _____.

9 Leonardo DiCaprio is a famous _____.

10 This person has a very small part in a film.

Down

1 Steven Spielberg was the _____ of the film *Jaws*.

2 These are the special clothes that an actor wears in a film.

3 In *The Wizard of Oz*, Judy Garland was the _____ Dorothy.

4 Tom Hanks was the _____ of the film *Forrest Gump*.

5 The paper that says you agree to do something.

7 People make movies and TV shows here.

2 Complete these texts about two Hollywood film stars using
the words below.

actors, audiences, became, character, Charlie Chaplin, costume,
flowers, industry, movies, music, newspapers, owned, parts,
place, popular, Rudolph Valentino, sidewalk, story, world

_____ was an important person in the early film _____
and he was the star of many _____ Hollywood movies.
_____ across the world loved films like *Making a Living*
or *The Gold Rush* and they always laughed at his _____
'The Tramp'. The Tramp was famous for his _____ of a
small coat, big trousers and a black hat.

Of course, he wasn't only an actor, he wrote the _____
for many movies and he _____ a film studio too. Visitors
to Hollywood often look for his star on the _____ in the
famous *Hollywood Walk of Fame*.

_____ first arrived in Hollywood in 1917 and he found
small _____ in silent films. Then, in the 1920s he was in
famous _____ like *Blood and Sand*. Women all over the
_____ loved his dark hair and wonderful eyes! He soon
_____ one of the most famous _____ in the world and
there were pictures of him in all the _____.

He died on 23 August 1926 and he is now in the
Hollywood Forever Cemetery. Visitors often go to
this _____ and learn more about the famous _____ of
'the woman in black' – she went to the cemetery every
year on 23 August and put _____ on his name.

Choose a famous actor that you are interested in. Plan and
write a text about this person. Give it to another student in
your class to read.

3 Look at these newspaper headlines. What are they about? What year do they come from?

1 **'Bigger and better' hotel opens today**
2 **Audiences can't stay away from jazz talkie**
3 Stars in town for new award ceremony
4 **'First teenager' killed in road accident**
5 Movie lover buys famous shoes for $15,000
6 **Thousands visit world's biggest multiplex**

4 Copy the table. Look back at the book and make notes about the different films.

	The Squaw Man	Ben-Hur	Jaws	Titanic
Year it came out	1914			
Director	Cecil B. DeMille			
Type of film	Feature film			
How much it cost	15,000 dollars			
Why it is famous	It was the first Hollywood feature film			

Find out about another film. Give a talk to your class about it. These websites can help you:
www.filmsite.org
www.hollywoodsgoldenage.com

ABOUT THE AUTHOR

Janet Hardy-Gould is an experienced teacher, writer, and teacher trainer. She is married with two children and lives in the town of Lewes in the south of England. In her free time, she likes walking across the beautiful hills near her town and meeting friends in cafés for tea and cakes.

She has written and co-written about thirty books for OUP including many graded readers. Her Bookworms titles are *King Arthur* and *Henry VIII and his Six Wives*, and the Factfiles *Deserts*, *Marco Polo and the Silk Road*, *Chocolate*, and *San Francisco*. For Dominoes she has written *The Great Fire of London*, *Mulan*, *Sinbad*, *The Travels of Ibn Battuta*, *Sherlock Holmes: The Emerald Crown*, *Hercules*, *Ali Baba and the Forty Thieves*, and *Crying Wolf and Other Tales*.

Janet is a member of an international film club in her home town and she loves watching films in different languages from around the world. She's also very interested in the history of film, both in Europe and the United States. Her favorite old Hollywood movies are *Casablanca* with Humphrey Bogart and Ingrid Bergman, and *Some Like it Hot* with Tony Curtis, Jack Lemmon, and Marilyn Monroe.

OXFORD BOOKWORMS LIBRARY

Classics • Crime & Mystery • Factfiles • Fantasy & Horror
Human Interest • Playscripts • Thriller & Adventure
True Stories • World Stories

The OXFORD BOOKWORMS LIBRARY provides enjoyable reading in English, with a wide range of classic and modern fiction, non-fiction, and plays. It includes original and adapted texts in seven carefully graded language stages, which take learners from beginner to advanced level. An overview is given on the next pages.

All Stage 1 titles are available as audio recordings, as well as over eighty other titles from Starter to Stage 6. All Starters and many titles at Stages 1 to 4 are specially recommended for younger learners. Every Bookworm is illustrated, and Starters and Factfiles have full-colour illustrations.

The OXFORD BOOKWORMS LIBRARY also offers extensive support. Each book contains an introduction to the story, notes about the author, a glossary, and activities. Additional resources include tests and worksheets, and answers for these and for the activities in the books. There is advice on running a class library, using audio recordings, and the many ways of using Oxford Bookworms in reading programmes. Resource materials are available on the website <www.oup.com/elt/gradedreaders>.

The *Oxford Bookworms Collection* is a series for advanced learners. It consists of volumes of short stories by well-known authors, both classic and modern. Texts are not abridged or adapted in any way, but carefully selected to be accessible to the advanced student.

You can find details and a full list of titles in the *Oxford Bookworms Library Catalogue* and *Oxford English Language Teaching Catalogues*, and on the website <www.oup.com/elt/gradedreaders>.

THE OXFORD BOOKWORMS LIBRARY
GRADING AND SAMPLE EXTRACTS

STARTER • 250 HEADWORDS

present simple – present continuous – imperative –
can/cannot, must – going to (future) – simple gerunds …

Her phone is ringing – but where is it?

Sally gets out of bed and looks in her bag. No phone. She looks under the bed. No phone. Then she looks behind the door. There is her phone. Sally picks up her phone and answers it. *Sally's Phone*

STAGE 1 • 400 HEADWORDS

… past simple – coordination with and, but, or –
subordination with before, after, when, because, so …

I knew him in Persia. He was a famous builder and I worked with him there. For a time I was his friend, but not for long. When he came to Paris, I came after him – I wanted to watch him. He was a very clever, very dangerous man. *The Phantom of the Opera*

STAGE 2 • 700 HEADWORDS

… present perfect – will (future) – (don't) have to, must not, could –
comparison of adjectives – simple if clauses – past continuous –
tag questions – ask/tell + infinitive …

While I was writing these words in my diary, I decided what to do. I must try to escape. I shall try to get down the wall outside. The window is high above the ground, but I have to try. I shall take some of the gold with me – if I escape, perhaps it will be helpful later. *Dracula*

STAGE 3 • 1000 HEADWORDS

... should, may – present perfect continuous – *used to* – past perfect –
causative – relative clauses – indirect statements ...

Of course, it was most important that no one should see
Colin, Mary, or Dickon entering the secret garden. So Colin
gave orders to the gardeners that they must all keep away
from that part of the garden in future. *The Secret Garden*

STAGE 4 • 1400 HEADWORDS

... past perfect continuous – passive (simple forms) –
would conditional clauses – indirect questions –
relatives with *where/when* – gerunds after prepositions/phrases ...

I was glad. Now Hyde could not show his face to the world
again. If he did, every honest man in London would be proud
to report him to the police. *Dr Jekyll and Mr Hyde*

STAGE 5 • 1800 HEADWORDS

... future continuous – future perfect –
passive (modals, continuous forms) –
would have conditional clauses – modals + perfect infinitive ...

If he had spoken Estella's name, I would have hit him. I was so
angry with him, and so depressed about my future, that I could
not eat the breakfast. Instead I went straight to the old house.
Great Expectations

STAGE 6 • 2500 HEADWORDS

... passive (infinitives, gerunds) – advanced modal meanings –
clauses of concession, condition

When I stepped up to the piano, I was confident. It was as if I
knew that the prodigy side of me really did exist. And when I
started to play, I was so caught up in how lovely I looked that
I didn't worry how I would sound. *The Joy Luck Club*

BOOKWORMS
FACTFILES
STAGE 1

San Francisco

JANET HARDY-GOULD

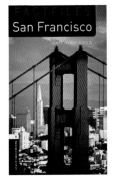

'It's a good place for gold,' said people in the 1840s, and they came from all over the world. 'It's a good place for a prison,' said the US government in the 1920s, and they put Al Capone there on the island of Alcatraz. 'It's a good place for love,' said the hippies in the 1960s, and they put flowers in their hair and came to Haight Ashbury. And San Francisco is still a good place – to take a hundred photographs, or see the Chinatown parade, or just to sit in a coffee shop and be in this interesting, different city . . .

BOOKWORMS
FACTFILES
STAGE 1

New York

JOHN ESCOTT

What can you do in New York? Everything! You can go to some of the world's most famous shops, watch a baseball game, go to the top of a skyscraper, see a concert in Central Park, eat a sandwich in a New York deli, see a show in a Broadway theater.

New York is big, noisy, and exciting, and it's waiting for you. Open the book and come with us to this wonderful city.